JUSTIFICATION

JUSTIFICATION
SINNERS RIGHTEOUS IN CHRIST

John Gill

'As by the offence of one judgment came upon all men to condemnation; even so by the righteousness of one the free gift came upon all men unto justification of life. For as by one man's disobedience many were made sinners, so by the obedience of one shall many be made righteous. Moreover the law entered, that the offence might abound. But where sin abounded, grace did much more abound: That as sin hath reigned unto death, even so might grace reign through righteousness unto eternal life by Jesus Christ our Lord' (*Romans 5: 18-21*)

GOSPEL STANDARD TRUST PUBLICATIONS

GOSPEL STANDARD TRUST PUBLICATIONS

12(b) Roundwood Lane, Harpenden, Hertfordshire, AL5 3DD, UK

2006

ISBN 10 : 1-897837-72-0
ISBN 13 : 978-1-897837-72-6

Printed by:
Olive Press Limited
73, The Green
Stotfold, Hitchin, Hertfordshire
SG5 4AN

Contents

Preface

Dear readers who seek the Lord, you who cannot be satisfied without the assurance of peace in your conscience, you who must have the Lord Jesus as your Friend, you who know you are unrighteous by nature and practice, we wish to give our reasons for publishing this work.

God's anger burns fiercely against sin. He has said that the soul that sins shall die and shall be cast out of his presence for ever into that place of eternal darkness and misery. We cannot cease from sin. We are born and shapen in it and we all shall die as sinners. What oppressive hopelessness and despair can fill our hearts. Is there no escape? Can we be delivered from this awful state and the distress that shadows us continually? Are we to die unrighteous and so receive the sentence from God our Judge to depart from him for ever? We cannot make ourselves righteous; we cannot rid ourselves of the burden of our sins; and so we cannot save ourselves from black despair.

We get our sin-bent nature from our father Adam. We share the guilt of his dreadful act of proud, ungodly, rebellious disobedience. We come under his condemnation that the moment he first sinned he would die and we, his children, with him. Being born his children, with his nature, we now add iniquity to iniquity as he did. We are verily guilty before our Creator. We are guilty in Adam's sin and through our own acts of sin. God has said that he will by no means clear the guilty.

But God did not execute the final sentence of eternal death on our father. He had more intentions towards Adam and his children than solely judgment for transgression. He purposed to show mercy and he communicated this intention and the means of its accomplishment through his faithful word in the Bible. We are told how God can execute his righteous judgment against sin and yet deliver the ungodly from hell. We are told how he, the holy unchanging God, can reckon an ungodly man to be perfectly righteous - that is, how he can justify the ungodly and receive them spotlessly sinless, yea, clothed in perfect righteousness, in his sight.

No wonder the angel said to the shepherds 'Fear not: for, behold, I bring you good tidings of great joy'. This Bible truth that God justifies the ungodly, is glad tidings of great joy to the sinner who languishes in distress, conscious of his ungodliness, and who thirsts to be accepted in the Lord Jesus Christ, who is the manifestation to us of the eternal invisible God, Father, Son and Holy Spirit.

All God's children, from the least to the greatest, are taught this great salvation. They are brought to thirst for it; they shall delight in it; they shall meditate upon it throughout eternity.

Just consider, this subject is so extensive and so relevant to each believer and to God's honour that the redeemed shall never tire throughout eternity of exploring its glories as centring in the Lamb of God. In this life, believers are given grace, wisdom unto salvation, according to the measure that God the Holy Spirit sovereignly purposes. In the world to come, all shall be given a fulness of understanding, a fulness of capacity to praise their Saviour.

The Lord has given to some men an anointing, an establishment in the truths of salvation, to act as under-shepherds to his little flock. In foretaste of the glorious occupation of the saints in glory, they are drawn to devote their lives to preaching Christ crucified, risen and glorified, as the One in whom men are justified and shall glory. They explore the breadth, length, depth and height of this salvation. They defend it against the incessant pressures of the devil whose heresies incline men to seek to justify themselves rather than submit to God's way of righteousness. John Gill (1697–1771), the Particular Baptist pastor who wrote this work, was such a defender of the faith.

John Gill's writings are very comprehensive in nature and include frequent references to the original languages and to the writings of other scholarly ministers of the gospel. Many students of God's truth, inclined to extensive reading, are familiar with Gill's Commentary of the whole Bible, his Body of Divinity, his Tracts and Sermons and other works. But many children of God, for various reasons, are not extensive readers. They can find the length and complexity of such writings as Gill's to be so daunting that they do not venture to read them. But John

Gill was a champion for the truths by which such persons are saved. He brought forth the glories, the riches of their saving justification by God. This is heavenly treasure. This is the foundation of their hopes for time and eternity. Only upon these truths can be grounded their assurance of eternal life. The work of the Holy Spirit is to lead the least of God's saints into the personal possession of this hope set before them in the gospel.

This extract from John Gill's Body of Divinity is directed towards those children of God who are not great readers and who are not familiar with his writings. We have tried to make this book as easy as possible for such to read. We have not changed Gill's words or the sequence of his paragraphs. But we have omitted many of the quotations which are in Hebrew and Greek. Of those that remain, their translation is either given by Gill in the text or inserted in square brackets by ourselves. The footnote references to other writers have been omitted, as most of their works will be inaccessible to our readers. We have included references in square brackets to more well-known writers such as John Owen and Thomas Goodwin.

Gill's sentences can be very long, with much use of semicolons and colons, but we have retained his punctuation. It was in the style of that day and the reader can come to appreciate its logic, flow and coherence. We have inserted our own headings to different sections of the book to break down the body of text into a more readable form and to emphasise the thread of Gill's thoughts. We have put spaces between his points to articulate them for the modern reader.

Gill's work was entitled 'A body of doctrinal and practical

divinity.' It is usually referred to as his 'Body of Divinity'. As the full title implies, he subdivided his work into two sections – doctrinal divinity and practical divinity. He further subdivided these into books.

The first part of our publication is from the doctrinal section, Book 2 titled 'Of the Acts and Works of God,' Chapter 5 'Of other Eternal and Immanent Acts of God, particularly Adoption and Justification.' We here only publish the section dealing with justification. An immanent act of God is one that is within himself. His determining from eternity to save sinners whom he had chosen was an eternal act within himself. God's eternal determinations are his immanent acts. In eternity the Father chose them and justified them in his Son. God eternally accounted them righteous in Christ. Gill opens up to believing sinners the glory of this doctrine, the certainty of their salvation, the comforting consideration that in their heavenly Father's view they have always been in a justifying union with Christ.

The second part of our publication is also from the doctrinal section, but Book 6 titled 'Of the Blessings of Grace, and the Doctrines of it,' Chapter 8 'Of Justification.' Here the author expounds the details of what justification is and how it is established in the consciences of believers. It is justification by faith rather than justification by works. This doctrine is at the heart of the gospel and was the foundational doctrine of the Reformation.

There is a long sermon by Gill, entitled 'The doctrine of justification by the righteousness of Christ stated and maintained.' We decided not to include this in the present publication because it has virtually the same content as his

Body of Divinity. If readers wish, they can obtain his works from Baptist Standard Bearer and Gospel Mission in the USA and from the Christian Bookshop, Ossett, in the UK.

We close with a sample quotation from our publication. Here you see the importance that the author attaches to this doctrine of justification and the sweetness he draws from it:

'The well-being of God's people here and hereafter depends upon their justification, and is a consequent of it; *Say ye to the righteous*, one that is justified by the righteousness of Christ, *that it shall be well with him* (*Isa. 3:10*), it is well with the justified ones in life; be it with them as it may, all is well with them and for the best; all things work together for their good, adversity and prosperity; what they have of worldly things, though but little (*Ps. 37:16; Prov. 15:16, 17*), are blessings to them: it is well with such an one at death, he has hope in it, and rejoices in hope of the glory of God; peace is the end of the perfect and upright man, who is perfectly righteous through the righteousness of Christ imputed to him; and it is well with him at judgment, he has a righteousness that will answer for him in that time to come; and he shall have an abundant entrance into the everlasting kingdom and glory of our Lord Jesus Christ; and it will be well with him to all eternity; he that is righteous will then be righteous still, and ever continue so, and shall go into everlasting life.'

Timothy Abbott
Committee member
Gospel Standard Trust

Part One

from

The Body of Divinity
Book 2: Of the acts and works of God
Chapter 5: Of other Eternal and Immanent Acts of God,
particularly Adoption and Justification
Section II: Justification

Justification from eternity

An internal and immanent act of God

THE SCOPE OF THIS PART OF THE WORK

Justification is an act of God's grace, flowing from his sovereign good will and pleasure; the elect of God are said to be *justified by his grace*; and as if that expression was not strong enough to set forth the freeness of it, the word *freely* is added elsewhere; *Being justified freely by his grace* (*Titus 3:7; Rom. 3:24*). Justification is by many divines distinguished into active and passive. Active justification is the act of God; it is God that justifies. Passive justification is the act of God, terminating on the conscience of a believer, commonly called a transient act, passing upon an external object. It is not of this I shall now treat [*see Part Two of this publication – Justification by Faith*], but of the former; which is an act internal and eternal, taken up in the divine mind from eternity, and is an immanent, abiding one in it; it is, as Dr. Ames expresses it, "a sentence conceived in the divine mind, by the decree of justifying."

Now, as before observed [*earlier in his Body of Doctrinal Divinity*], as God's will to elect, is the election of his people, so his will to justify them, is the justification of them; as it is an immanent act in God, it is an act of his grace towards them, is wholly without them, entirely resides in the divine mind, and lies in his estimating, accounting, and constituting them righteous, through the righteousness of his Son; and, as such, did not first commence in time, but from eternity.

(1) THE ELECT JUSTIFIED BEFORE ANY ACT OF FAITH

First, It does not begin to take place in time, or at believing, but is antecedent to any act of faith.

Faith not the cause but the effect of justification

1. Faith is not the cause, but an effect of justification; it is not the cause of it in any sense; it is not the moving cause, that is the free grace of God; *Being justified freely by his grace* (*Rom. 3:24*), nor the efficient cause of it; *It is God that justifies* (*Rom. 8:33*), nor the meritorious cause, as some express it; or the matter of it, that is the obedience and blood of Christ (*Rom. 5:9, 19*), or the righteousness of Christ, consisting of his active and passive obedience; nor even the instrumental cause; for, as Mr. Baxter himself argues, "If faith is the instrument of our justification, it is the instrument either of God or man; not of man, for justification is God's act; he is the sole Justifier (*Rom. 3:26*), man doth not justify himself:

nor of God, for it is not God that believes": nor is it a *causa sine qua non*, as the case of elect infants shows; it is not in any class of causes whatever; but it is the effect of justification: all men have not faith, and the reason why some do not believe is, because they are none of Christ's sheep; they were not chosen in him, nor justified through him; but justly left in their sins, and so to condemnation; the reason why others believe is, because they are ordained to eternal life, have a justifying righteousness provided for them, and are justified by it, and shall never enter into condemnation: the reason why any are justified, is not because they have faith; but the reason why they have faith, is because they are justified; was there no such blessing of grace as justification of life in Christ, for the sons of men, there would be no such thing as faith in Christ bestowed on them; precious faith is obtained through the righteousness of our God and Saviour Jesus Christ (*2 Peter 1:1*), nor, indeed, would there be any room for it, nor any use of it, if a justifying righteousness was not previously provided. Agreeable to this are the reasonings and assertions of Twisse, Maccovius, and others. Now if faith is not the cause, but the effect of justification; then as every cause is before its effect, and every effect follows its cause, justification must be before faith, and faith must follow justification.

Faith the evidence of justification

2. Faith is the evidence and manifestation of justification, and therefore justification must be before it; *Faith is the evidence of things not seen* (*Heb. 11:1*), but it is not the evidence of that which as yet is not; what it is an evidence of, must be, and

it must exist before it. *The righteousness of God*, of the God-man and mediator Jesus Christ, *is revealed from faith to faith*, in the everlasting gospel (*Rom. 1:17*), and therefore must be before it is revealed, and before faith, to which it is revealed: faith is that grace whereby a soul, having seen its guilt, and its want of righteousness, beholds, in the light of the divine Spirit, a complete righteousness in Christ, renounces its own, lays hold on that, puts it on as a garment, rejoices in it, and glories of it; the Spirit of God witnessing to his spirit, that he is a justified person; and so he is evidently and declaratively *justified in the name of the Lord Jesus, and by the Spirit of our God* (*1 Cor. 6:11*).

Faith adds nothing to the essence of justification

3. Faith adds nothing to the *esse* only to the *bene esse* of justification; it is no part of, nor any ingredient in it; it is a complete act in the eternal mind of God, without the being or consideration of faith, or any foresight of it; a man is as much justified before as after it, in the account of God; and after he does believe, his justification does not depend on his acts of faith; for though *we believe not, yet he abides faithful (2 Tim. 2:13)* ; that is, God is faithful to his covenant engagements with his Son, as their Surety, by whose suretyship righteousness they are justified; but by faith men have a comfortable sense, perception and apprehension of their justification, and enjoy that peace of soul which results from it; it is by that only, under the testimony of the divine Spirit, that they know their interest in it, and can claim it, and so have the comfort of it.

Justification must exist before faith can receive it

4. But justification is the object, and faith the act that is conversant with it. Now every object is prior to the act that is concerned with it; unless when an act gives being to the object, which is not the case here; for faith, as has been seen, is not the cause, nor matter of justification; what the eye is to the body, that is faith to the soul: the eye, by virtue of its visive faculty, beholds sensible objects, but does not produce them; they are before they are seen, and did they not previously exist, the eye could not behold them; the sun is before it is seen; and so in innumerable other instances: faith is to the soul, as the hand is to the body, receives things for its use; but then these things must be before they are received; faith receives the blessing of justification from the Lord, even that righteousness by which it is justified, from the God of its salvation; but then this blessing must exist before faith can receive it (*Ps. 24:5*). Christ's righteousness, by which men are justified, is compared to a robe or garment, which faith puts on; but then as a garment must be wrought and completely made, before it is put on, so must the justifying righteousness of Christ be, before it can be put on by faith.

The elect justified in Christ before they believe

5. All the elect of God were justified in Christ, their Head and Representative, when he rose from the dead, and therefore they believe: Christ engaged as a Surety for all his people from eternity, had their sins imputed to him, and for which he made himself responsible; in the fulness of time he made satisfaction for them by his sufferings and death, and at his resurrection

was acquitted and discharged: now as he suffered and died, not as a private, but as a public person, so he rose again, and was justified as such, even as the representative of his people; hence when he rose, they rose with him; and when he was justified, they were justified in him; for he was *delivered for their offences, and was raised again for their justification* (*Rom. 4:25; see 1 Tim. 3:16*), and this is the sense and judgment of many sound and learned divines; as, besides our Sandford and Dr. Goodwin, the learned Amesius, Hoornbeck, Witsius, and others.

(2) JUSTIFICATION IS FROM ETERNITY

Secondly, Justification is not only before faith, but it is from eternity, being an immanent act in the divine mind, and so an internal and eternal one; as may be concluded:-

Election and hence justification is from eternity

1. From eternal election: the objects of justification are God's elect; *Who shall lay anything to the charge of God's elect? it is God that justifies*; that is, the elect. Now if God's elect, as such, can have nothing laid to their charge; but are by God acquitted, discharged, and justified; and if they bore this character of elect from eternity, or were chosen in Christ before the world began; then they must be acquitted, discharged and justified so early, so as nothing could be laid to their charge: besides, by electing grace men were put into Christ, and were considered as in him before the foundation of the world; and if they were considered as in him, they must be considered as

righteous or unrighteous; not surely as unrighteous, unjustified, and in a state of condemnation; for *there is no condemnation to them which are in Christ (Rom. 8:1)*, and therefore must be considered as righteous, and so justified: "Justified then we were, says Dr. Goodwin, when first elected, though not in our own persons, yet in our Head, as he had our persons then given him, and we came to have a being and an interest in him."

Justification a branch of election

2. Justification may well be considered as a branch of election; it is no other, as one expresses it, than setting apart the elect alone to be partakers of Christ's righteousness; and a setting apart Christ's righteousness for the elect only; it is mentioned along with election, as of the same date with it; *Wherein*, that is, in the grace of God, particularly the electing grace of God, spoken of before, *he hath made us accepted in the beloved (Eph. 1:6)*. What is this acceptance in Christ, but justification in him? and this is expressed as a past act, in the same language as other eternal things be in the context, he *hath* blessed us, and he *hath* chosen us, and *having* predestinated us, so he *hath* made us accepted; and, indeed, as Christ was always the beloved of God, and well pleasing to him; so all given to him, and in him, were beloved of God, well pleasing to him, and accepted with him, or justified in him from eternity.

Justification one of the 'all spiritual blessings'

3. Justification is one of those spiritual blessings wherewith the elect are blessed in Christ according to election-grace, before the foundation of the world (*Eph. 1:3, 4*). That

justification is a spiritual blessing none will deny; and if the elect were blessed with all spiritual blessings, then with this; and if thus blessed according to election, or when elected, then before the foundation of the world: and this grace of justification must be no small part of that *grace which was given in Christ Jesus before the foundation of the world was* (*2 Tim. 1:9*). "We may say," says Dr. Goodwin, "of all spiritual blessings in Christ, what is said of Christ, that *his goings forth are from everlasting*—in Christ we were blessed with all spiritual blessings (*Eph. 1:3*), as we are blessed with all other, so with this also, that we were justified then in Christ!"

The elect justified in Christ as their surety from everlasting

4. Christ became a Surety for his people from everlasting; engaged to pay their debts, bear their sins, and make satisfaction for them; and was accepted of as such by God his Father, who thenceforward looked at him for payment and satisfaction, and looked at them as discharged, and so they were in his eternal mind; and it is a rule that will hold good, as Maccovius observes, "that as soon as one becomes a surety for another, the other is immediately freed, if the surety be accepted;" which is the case here and it is but a piece of common prudence, when a man has a bad debt, and has good security for it, to look not to the principal debtor, who will never be able to pay him, but to his good bondsman and surety, who is able; and so Dr. Goodwin observes, that God, in the everlasting transaction with Christ, "told him, as it were, that he would look for his debt and satisfaction of him, and that he did let the sinners go free; and so they are in this respect, justified from all eternity."

From eternity, sin not imputed to the elect

5. The everlasting transaction, the same excellent writer thinks, is imported in 2 Corinthians 5:19. *God was in Christ reconciling the world unto himself, not imputing their trespasses unto them.* And Witsius is of opinion, "that this act of God may be called, the general justification of the elect."

And, indeed, since it was the determination of God, and the scheme and method he proposed to take in Christ for the reconciliation of the elect, not to impute their sins to them, but to his Son, their Surety; then seeing they are not imputed to them, but to him; and if reckoned and accounted to him, then not to them; and if charged to him, then they must be discharged from them, and so justified; and a non-imputation of sin to the elect, is no other than a justification of them; and thus the apostle strongly concludes the imputation of Christ's righteousness; which is the *formalis ratio*, or the form of justification, from the non-imputation of sin, and the remission of it (*Rom. 4:6-8*).

God's eternal will to punish Christ for the sins of the elect

6. It was the will of God from everlasting, not to punish sin in the persons of his elect, but to punish it in the person of Christ; and that it was his will not to punish it in his people, but in his Son, is manifest from his setting him forth in his purposes and decrees, to be the propitiation for sin; and from his sending him forth in the likeness of sinful flesh, to condemn sin in the flesh; and from his being made sin and a curse, that his people might be made the righteousness of God in him. Now, as has been often observed, no new will can arise in God; God wills nothing in time, but what he willed from eternity; and if it was the

eternal will of God not to punish sin in his people, but in his Son, then they were eternally discharged, acquitted from sin, and secured from everlasting wrath and destruction; and if they were eternally discharged from sin, and freed from punishment, they were eternally justified: Dr. Twisse makes the very quiddity and essence of justification and remission of sin, which he takes to be the same, to lie in the will of God not to punish; and asserts, that this will not to punish, as it is an immanent act, was from eternity.

God justified Old Testament believers before Christ came

7. It deserves regard and attention, that the saints under the Old Testament, were justified by the same righteousness of Christ, as those under the New, and that before the sacrifice was offered up, the satisfaction given, and the everlasting righteousness brought in; for Christ's blood was shed for the remission of sins that were past, and his death was for the redemption of transgressions under the first Testament (*Rom. 3:25; Heb. 9:15*). Now if God could, and actually did, justify some, three or four thousand years before the righteousness of Christ was actually wrought out, taking his Son's word and bond as their Surety, and in a view of his future righteousness; why could he not, and why may it not be thought he did, justify all his elect from eternity, upon the word and bond of their Surety, and on the foot of his future righteousness, which he had engaged to work out, and which he full well knew he would most certainly work out? and if there is no difficulty in conceiving of the one, there can be none in conceiving of the other.

(3) OBJECTIONS TO THIS DOCTRINE

There are many objections made to this truth; some are so trifling as to deserve no notice; a few of the more principal ones I shall briefly answer to, and chiefly those made, for the most part, by the learned Turretine.

Men cannot be justified before they exist?

1. It is objected, that men cannot be justified before they exist; they must be, before they can be justified; since *non entis nulla sunt accidentia*", &c. of a nonentity nothing can be said, nor anything ascribed to it. To which I answer, whatever is in this objection, lies as strongly against eternal election, as against eternal justification; for it may as well be said, how can a man be elected before he exists? he must be before he can be chosen, or be the object of choice. I own, with Maccovius, that this is true of nonentities, that have neither an *esse actu*, nor an *esse cognitum*, that have neither an actual being, nor is it certain, nor known that they shall have any future being: but though God's elect have not an actual being from eternity, yet it is certain, by the prescience and predetermination of God, that they shall have one; for *known unto God are all his works from the beginning*, or from eternity (*Acts 15:18*). And besides this, they have an *esse representativum*, a representative being in Christ; which is more than other creatures have, whose future existences are certain; even such a being as makes them capable of being chosen in Christ, and blessed in him before the foundation of the world, and of having grace given them in him before the world was; and why not then of being justified in him? (*Eph. 1:3, 4; 2 Tim. 1:9*).

Moreover, as the same writer observes, "Justification is a moral act, which does not require the existence of the subject together with it; but it is enough that it shall exist some time or other."

Men cannot be justified before they have committed sin?

2. It is further objected, that if God's elect are justified from eternity, then they were not only justified before they themselves existed, but before any sin was committed by them; and it seems absurd that men should be justified from sins before they were committed, or any charge of them brought against them. To which may be replied, that it is no more absurd to say, that God's elect were justified from their sins before they were committed, than it is to say, that they were imputed to Christ, and he died for them, and made satisfaction for them before committed; which is most certainly true of all those that live, since the coming and death of Christ: such that believe the doctrines of the imputation of sin to Christ, and of his satisfaction for it, ought never to make this objection; and if they do, they ought to be fully content with the answer. As for the charge of sin against God's elect, that is not first made when brought to the conscience of an awakened sinner; justice brought the charge against all the elect, in the eternal transactions between the Father and the Son; or how came Christ to be bail and Surety for them? or how otherwise could there be a transfer of the charge from them to Christ? and where is the grace of a non-imputation of sin to them, and of an imputation of it to Christ, if it was not imputable to them, and chargeable on them?

The decree to justify cannot be actual justification?

3. It is urged, that strictly and accurately speaking, it cannot be said that justification is eternal, because the decree of justification is one thing, and justification itself another; even as God's will of sanctifying is one thing, and sanctification itself another; wherefore, though the decree of justification is eternal, and precedes faith, that itself is in time, and follows it. To which it may be answered, that as God's decree and will to elect men to everlasting life and salvation, is his election of them; and his will not to impute sin to them, is the non-imputation of it; and his will to impute the righteousness of Christ unto them, is the imputation of it to them; so his decree, or will to justify them, is the justification of them, as that is an immanent act in God; which has its complete essence in his will, as election has; is entirely within himself, and not transient on an external subject, producing any real, physical, inherent change in it, as sanctification is and does; and therefore the case is not alike: it is one thing for God to will to act an act of grace concerning men, another thing to will to work a work of grace in them; in the former case, the will of God is his act of justification; in the latter it is not his act of sanctification; wherefore, though the will of God to justify, is justification itself, that being a complete act in his eternal mind, without men; yet his will to sanctify, is not sanctification, because that is a work wrought in men, and not only requires the actual existence of them but an exertion of powerful and efficacious grace upon them: was justification, as the papists say, by an infusion of inherent righteousness in men, there would be some strength in the objection; but this is not the case, and therefore there is none in it.

Calling put before justification in Romans 8:30?

4. It is observed, that the apostle, reckoning up in order, the benefits which flow from the love of God to the elect, in his famous chain of salvation, sets calling before justification, as something antecedent to it (*Rom. 8:30*), from whence it is concluded, that calling is in order of time, before justification. To which I reply, that the order of things in scripture is frequently inverted. The Jews have a saying, that there is nothing prior and posterior in the law; that is, that the order of things is not strictly observed; to put that first which is first, and that last which is last; but the order is changed, and therefore nothing strictly can be concluded from thence; even the order of persons in the Trinity is not always kept to, sometimes the Son is placed before the Father, and the Holy Spirit before them both; which, though it may be improved into an argument for their equality, yet not to destroy the order among them; and so with respect to calling, it may be observed, that it is sometimes placed before election (*2 Peter 1:10*), but none but an Arminian would argue from thence, that it is really before it in order of time, or that men are not elected until they are called: on the other hand, salvation is placed before calling (*2 Tim. 1:9*). *Who hath saved us, and called us*, &c. from whence we might, with as great propriety, argue, that salvation, and so justification, precedes calling; as to argue, from the other text in Romans, that calling precedes justification, in order of time. Indeed, nothing is to be concluded with certainty, one way or another, from such modes and forms of expression. Justification, as a transient act, and declarative, follows calling; but as an immanent act

in God, it goes before it, of which we are only speaking, as ought always to be remembered.

If justified by faith, then faith a prerequisite of justification?

5. It is affirmed, that those various passages of scripture, where we are said to be justified through faith, and by faith, have no other tendency than to show that faith is something prerequisite to justification, which cannot be said if justification was from eternity. To which the answer is, that those scriptures which speak of justification, through and by faith, do not militate against, nor disprove justification before faith; for though justification by and before faith differ, yet they are not opposite and contradictory. They differ, the one being an immanent act in God; all which sort of acts are eternal, and so before faith; the other being a transient declarative act, terminating on the conscience of the believer; and so is by and through faith, and follows it. But then these do not contradict each other, the one being a declaration and manifestation of the other. What scriptures may be thought to speak of faith, as a prerequisite to justification, cannot be understood as speaking of it as a prerequisite to the being of justification; for faith has no causal influence upon it, it adds nothing to its being, it is no ingredient in it, it is not the cause nor matter of it; at most, they can only be understood as speaking of faith as a prerequisite to the knowledge and comfort of it, and to a claim of interest in it; and this is readily allowed, that no man is evidentially and declaratively justified until he believes; that is, he cannot have the knowledge of it, nor any comfort from it; nor can he claim his interest in it, without faith; and this being observed, obviates

another objection, that if justification is before faith, then faith is needless and useless. It is not so; it is not of use to justify men, which it is never said to do; but it is of use to receive the blessing of justification, and to enjoy the comfort of it.

Justified before believing, yet by nature children of wrath?

6. It is asserted, that justification cannot be from eternity, but only in time, when a man actually believes and repents; otherwise it would follow, that he who is justified, and consequently has passed from death to life, and is become a child of God, and an heir of eternal life, abides still in death, and is a child of wrath, because he who is not yet converted, and lies in sin, abides in death (*1 John 3:14*), and is of the devil (*1 John 3:8*), and in a state of damnation (*Gal. 5:21*), but this latter especially cannot be admitted of, with respect to God's elect, even while unconverted. And now, to remove this seeming difficulty, let it be observed, that the elect of God may be considered under two different *heads*, Adam and Christ, and as related to two covenants at one and the same time; as they are the descendants of Adam, they are related to him as a covenant head, and as such, sinned in him, and judgment came upon them all to condemnation and death, and so they are, by nature, children of wrath, even as others. But as considered in Christ, they are loved with an everlasting love, chosen in him before the world was, and always viewed and accounted righteous in him, and so secured from everlasting wrath and damnation; hence it is no contradiction to say, that the elect of God, as in Adam, and according to the covenant of works, are under the sentence of condemnation; and that as in

Christ, and according to the covenant of grace, and the secret transactions thereof, they are justified, and saved from condemnation. This is no more a contradiction, than that they were loved with an everlasting love, and yet are children of wrath, at one and the same time, as they most certainly are; nor than that Jesus Christ was the object of his Father's love and wrath at the same time, he sustaining two different capacities, and standing in two different relations, when he suffered in the room and stead of his people; as the Son of God he was always the object of his love; as the Surety of his people, bearing their sins, and suffering for them, he was the object of his wrath (*Ps. 89:38*).

If 'now justified' (1 Cor. 6:11) then not justified before?

7. It is urged what the apostle says (*1 Cor. 6:11*). *Now ye are justified*; as if they were not justified before; but the word now is not in the text; and was it, and admit that to be the sense of it, it does not follow that they were not justified before: for so they might be *in foro dei*, in the court of God, and in his account from eternity, and in Christ their Head and Surety, and especially when he rose from the dead, before now; yet not till now be justified in *foro conscientiae*, in their own consciences, and by the Spirit of God; which is the justification the apostle is there speaking of. In a word, the sentence of justification pronounced on Christ, the representative of his people, when he rose from the dead, and that which is pronounced by the Spirit of God in the consciences of believers, and that which will be pronounced before men and angels at the general judgment, are only so many repetitions, or renewed declarations,

of that grand original sentence of it, conceived in the mind of God from all eternity; which is the eternal justification pleaded for; and is no other than what many eminent divines of the highest character for learning and judgment, have asserted, as before observed; and it is to such as these Dr. Owen refers [in his Doctrine of Justification vindicated from the animadversions of Richard Baxter p. 9], when he replied to Mr. Baxter, who charged him with holding eternal justification; "I neither am, nor ever was of that judgement; though as it may be explained, I know better, wiser, and more learned men than myself, (and he might have added, than Mr. Baxter,) that have been, and are."

Part Two

from

The Body of Divinity
Book 6: Of the blessings of grace, and the doctrines of it
Chapter 8: Of justification

Justification by faith

Justification as it terminates in the conscience of a believer

PARDON AND JUSTIFICATION

Pardon of sin, and justification from it, are very closely connected; the one follows upon the other; according to the position of them in some passages of scripture, pardon is first, and justification next (*as in Acts 13:38, 39; 26:18*); though they are not, the one, in reality, prior to the other; they are both together in the divine mind, and in the application of them to the conscience of a sinner; indeed, according to the order of causes, justification by the righteousness of Christ, imputed, may be considered as before pardon; since God forgives sin for Christ's sake; that is, for the sake of his righteousness imputed. Now that for the sake of which a thing is, must be before that for which it is, as the cause is before the effect. Some take them to be the same, and that justification lies solely in the remission of sins; and others more rightly make the imputation of Christ's righteousness, and forgiveness of sins, the two parts of justification, distinct ones; while others think they are not two integral parts, really distinct, but only one act, respecting two terms; just as by one and the same act, darkness is expelled from the air, and light is introduced; so by one and the same act of justification, the sinner is absolved from guilt, and pronounced righteous; hence they suppose such express the whole of justification, who say, it consists in the remission of sins, and those that say it consists in the imputation of righteousness; because when God forgives men their sins, he pronounces them righteous, through the imputation of Christ's righteousness to them; and when he pronounces them righteous, by that he forgives them their sins; remission of sin supposes the imputation of Christ's righteousness; and the imputation of Christ's righteousness infers the remission of sin. But though these are not to be separated, yet they are to be distinguished; and I should choose to consider them, not as distinct parts of the same thing, but as distinct blessings of grace; for though pardon and justification agree in some things, in others they differ. In some things they agree.

Wherein pardon and justification agree

1. In their efficient cause, God: as God only can and does forgive sin, it is his prerogative, it is peculiar to him; so it is God that justifies the sinner, and he only; *there is one God, who justifies the circumcision by faith, and the uncircumcision through faith*; that is, that justifies both Jews and Gentiles, who believe in Christ (*Mark 2:7; Rom. 3:30*).

2. In their moving cause, the free grace of God: pardon of sin is owing to the riches of God's grace, and the multitude of his tender mercy; and justification is ascribed to the grace of God, and is said to be freely by his grace (*Eph 1:7; Ps. 51:1; Titus 3:7; Rom. 3:24*).

3. In their procuring cause, the blood of Christ: the blood of Christ was shed to procure the remission of sins, and it is by it; and so likewise justification is by the same blood (*Matt. 26:28; Rom. 5:9*).

4. In the objects of it: the same persons that are pardoned are justified, and the same that are justified are pardoned; to whom God imputes the righteousness of Christ, to their justification, to them he gives the remission of sin; and to whom he does not impute sin, but forgives it, he imputes righteousness without works (*Rom. 4:6-8*).

5. In their commencement and completion: pardon and justification commence together, and both are finished at once; and are not carried on in a gradual and progressive way, as sanctification is[1] (*Col. 2:13; Acts 13:39*).

6. In the manner of actual enjoying them, which is in a way of receiving, and that by faith; it is by faith men receive the forgiveness of sins; and by it they receive abundance of grace, and the gift of righteousness to justification of life; and, this is

---

[1]*But see author's reference on page 70 to Christ being our sanctification*

what the Scriptures call justification by faith (*Acts 26:18; Rom. 5:1, 17, 18*).

But though they [i.e. pardon and justification] agree in these things, in others they differ.

Wherein pardon and justification differ

1. Pardon is of men that are sinners, and who remain such, and may be called so, though pardoned sinners; but justification is a pronouncing persons righteous, as if they had never sinned; it is one thing for a man to be arraigned at the bar as a criminal, and be tried, cast, and condemned, and after that be pardoned; and another thing for a man to be tried by law, and to be found and declared righteous by it, as though he had not transgressed it.

2. Pardon takes away sin from the sinner, but does not give him a righteousness, as justification does; pardon takes away the filthy garments; but it is justification that clothes with change of raiment, with the robe of Christ's righteousness; these are two distinct things (*Zech. 3:4*).

3. Pardon frees from punishment, and an obligation to it, as it takes away guilt; *the Lord hath put away thy sin; thou shalt not die* (*2 Sam. 12:13*), but does not entitle to everlasting life, happiness, and glory: that justification does, and therefore is called *justification of life*; and in consequence of which men are *made heirs according to the hope of eternal life* (*Rom. 5:18; Titus 3:7*). When a king pardons a criminal, he does not by that act entitle him to an estate, much less to his crown and kingdom; but

[40]

if he will, when he has pardoned him, take him to court, and make him his son and heir, it must be by another distinct act of royal favour.

4. More is required for justification than for pardon; the blood of Christ was sufficient to procure pardon, and did procure it: but to the justification of a sinner, the holiness of the human nature of Christ, the perfect obedience of his life, and his bloodshed, and sufferings of death, are and must be imputed.

5. The righteousness of Christ, by which men are justified, is the fulfilling of the law; Christ came to fulfil it in the room of his people; and he is the fulfilling end of it to them, for righteousness; which is inherent in him, the author of it: not so pardon; that does not fulfil the law, gives no righteousness; nor does it reside in Christ, as righteousness does (*Rom. 10:4; Isa. 45:24*).

6. Pardon lies in the non-imputation of sin; justification in the imputation of righteousness: righteousness is imputed, but pardon is not (*Rom. 4:6,7*).

7. Justification passed on Christ, as the head and representative of his people; but not pardon: Christ having had the sins of his people imputed to him, and having made satisfaction to the justice of God for them, he was acquitted, discharged, and justified; but not pardoned: we may truly say, Christ was justified, and that God justified him, because the Scriptures say so; but not that he was pardoned; such an expression would sound harsh, and be very unwarrantable (*see Isa 50:8, 9; 1 Tim. 3:16*).

8. An innocent person, falsely charged, may be acquitted and justified, when he cannot be said to be pardoned; yea, such who need no pardon, as Adam did not in his state of innocence, and the elect angels in heaven; yet may be said to be justified, that is declared to be just and righteous: so men, in the present state, could they perfectly fulfil the law, as they cannot, would be justified by it; *for the doers of the law are justified; he that does these things shall live by them* (*Rom. 2:13; 10:5*). Moreover, if justification and pardon are to be considered as cause and effect, as before observed, they must be distinct, and are not to be confounded.

Importance of the doctrine of justification

The doctrine of justification by the righteousness of Christ is a doctrine of great importance; the apostle speaks of it as if the essence of the gospel lay in it; and calls the opposite to it, justification by the works of the law, another gospel (*see Gal. 1:6,7; 3:8*); it is a fundamental article of the gospel; some have called it, the *basis* of Christianity; it was the great doctrine of the reformation; what our first reformers made their chief study; and by it cut the sinews of popery, the antichristian doctrines of penance and purgatory, of pardons and indulgences, of the merit of good works, works of supererogation, &c. Luther used to call it, *articulus stantis vel cedentis ecclesiae,* the article of the church, by which it stands or falls; as this is, the church is; if this obtains, the church is in a well settled and prosperous state; but if this loses ground, and is rejected, it is in a ruinous one: if this is a rule to judge by, it may be easily discerned, in what case the church, and interest of religion, now are. This doctrine is the ground and foundation of all solid joy, peace, and comfort, in this life, and hope of eternal glory hereafter.

I have, in a former part of this work, [*See Part One – Justification from eternity*], treated of justification, as an immanent and eternal act in God; and so it may be said to be from eternity, and before faith; and in what sense it is so, with a removal of objections, has been shown in the place referred to; and therefore shall only now discourse concerning justification, as it terminates in the conscience of a believer; and which the scriptures style justification by faith.

(1) WHAT IS THE ACT OF JUSTIFICATION

I shall, *firstly,* consider the act of justification, and in what sense the word is to be taken. And,

What justification is not

1. It is not to be understood of instructing men in the scheme and method of justification, whether in a legal or evangelical way (*Acts 15:1; 1 Tim. 1:7; Dan. 12:3*).

2. Nor is it to be understood of making men righteous, by infusing righteousness into them; for this is to confound justification and sanctification together, which are two distinct things (*1 Cor. 1:30; 6:11*), this is sanctification: the righteousness by which men are justified, is imputed to them; but the righteousness of sanctification is inherent in them; that by which men are justified, are the obedience and blood of Christ; but infused holiness is neither of these.

The word *justify* is never used in a physical sense, for producing any real internal change in men; but in a forensic sense, and stands opposed, not to a state of impurity and unholiness, but to a state of condemnation; it is a law term, and used of judicial affairs, transacted in a court of judicature (*see Deut. 25:1; Prov. 17:15; Isa. 5:23; Matthew 12:37*), where justification stands opposed to condemnation; and this is the sense of the word whenever it is used in the doctrine under consideration; so in Job 9:2, 3 and 25:4 so by David (*Ps. 143:2*), and in all Paul's epistles, where the doctrine of justification is treated of, respect is had to courts of judicature, and to a judicial process in them; men are represented as sinners, charged with sin, and pronounced guilty before God, and subject to condemnation and death; when, according to this evangelic doctrine, they are justified by the obedience and blood of Christ, cleared of all charges, acquitted and absolved, and freed from condemnation and death, and adjudged to eternal life (*see Rom. 3:9, 19; 5:9, 16, 18, 19; 8:1, 33, 34; Gal. 2:16, 17; Titus 3:7*).

What justification is

3. Justification is to be understood in this doctrine, not of justification before men, before whom men may appear righteous (*Matt. 23:28*), but in the sight of God, in whose sight they cannot be justified by the works of the law (*Rom. 3:20*). Nor of the justification of a man's cause; or of his vindication from the calumnies of men (*1 Sam. 12:3-6; Ps. 7:8; Job 13:18*). Nor of the justification of a man's faith by his works, thereby proving the genuineness and sincerity of it: so

the faith of Abraham, and of Rahab, was justified by their works; or their faith in the promises made unto them, was proved to be genuine and sincere; the one by offering up his son; and the other by hiding the spies (*Jas. 2:21-25*). But of the justification of the persons of men before God; and this is either legal or evangelical: legal, on condition of a person's fulfilling the whole law, or yielding perfect obedience to it; which, in man's present state and circumstances, is impossible (*Rom. 2:13; 10:5; 8:3, 4*). Evangelical, which is an act of God's grace, accounting and pronouncing a person righteous, through the righteousness of Christ imputed to him, and received by faith; so *by the obedience of one many are made righteous*; and, Christ is of God, *made righteousness to them*; and they are *made the righteousness of God in him*; are reckoned perfectly righteous through him, and so stand justified and accepted in the sight of God (*Rom. 5:19; 1 Cor. 1:30; 2 Cor. 5:21*), and this is the justification we are treating of; concerning which further observe,

(2) GOD IS THE CAUSE OR SPRING OF JUSTIFICATION

The causes of it. The *moving cause* is the grace of God; it was the sovereign grace, favour, and goodwill of God, which put him upon forming the scheme and method of justification; which moved him to appoint and send his Son, to work out, and bring in a righteousness for the justification of his people; and then to accept of it as their justifying righteousness, and to impute it freely to them, without works: the procuring, meritorious, or material cause of justification, is the righteousness of Christ imputed, which will be treated of more largely, when we come to consider the matter of justification; or what that is, for the sake of which, any of the sons of men are justified before God. At present, I shall only attend to the *efficient* cause of justification, who is God; *It is God that justifies* (*Rom. 8:33; 3:26, 30; Gal. 3:8*), which is marvellous; since,

Marvellous that it is God who justifies!

1. He is the Judge of all the earth, who will do right, and will by no means clear the guilty. Judges among men, by his orders and instructions, and as they would forfeit his displeasure, were not to justify the wicked; and yet he, who is Judge himself in the earth, *justifies the ungodly*: but then it should be observed, that he does not justify them without a righteousness, but upon the foot of Christ's righteousness; so that though he justifies the ungodly, yet not as ungodly, but as righteous, through the righteousness of his Son; hence it is, that it is one of the privileges of such persons, that they can *come to God, the Judge of all*, without fear and dread, appearing before him perfectly righteous in Christ the Mediator (*Heb. 12:23, 24*).

2. Whose law is the rule by which he judges, and that law broken by men, and yet he justifies them. The law is holy, just, and good, and requires perfect, sinless obedience of men, but is broken by them in ten thousand instances; and he that offends in one point, is guilty of all, and the law pronounces him guilty, and curses and condemns him; and yet God, who judges according to this law, justifies them (*Rom. 2:12*), but then it should be observed, that Christ has fulfilled the law, in the

room and stead of these persons; so that *the righteousness of the law* is said to be *fulfilled in them*; and it is considered as if it was fulfilled by them; and on this account they are legally acquitted, discharged, and justified, according to this law; its demands being fully satisfied by Christ.

3. Sin, the breach of the law of God, is committed against him, and is hateful to him, and yet he justifies from it; every sin, being a transgression of the law, is against God, the Lawgiver, and cannot but be resented by him, and be an abomination to him; he hates it, and the workers of it; well then might Bildad say, *How then can man be justified with God? (Job 25:4)*, and yet he is.

4. It is that God that justifies, who will not admit of an imperfect righteousness, in the room of a perfect one: man's righteousness is imperfect, and cannot be reckoned as a perfect one by him, whose judgment is according to truth; nor will it stand in judgment, nor answer for the sinner at the bar of God, and justify in his sight; and yet God justifies; but then it is through the perfect righteousness of Christ, who is *the end of the law for righteousness to everyone that believes (Rom. 10:4)*.

5. That God, who is the Lawgiver, and is able to save and to destroy, who has the power to destroy both body and soul in hell, and would be just in so doing, and into whose hands it is a fearful thing to fall, yet he justifies. Now this act of justification, as ascribed to God, belongs to all the three Persons in the Godhead; they are all concerned in it, Father, Son, and Spirit.

God the Father justifies

First, God the Father; who, in many places where he is spoken of as a justifier, is distinguished from Christ; as where it is said, *It is God that justifieth—who shall condemn? It is Christ that died!* Again, God is said to *be just, and the justifier of him that believeth in Jesus* (*Rom. 8:34; 3:25, 26*), the same that justifies the head, justifies the members; now it is the Father that justified Christ, the head of his elect, of whom Christ says, *He is near that justifieth me* (*Isa. 50:8*).

1. God the Father contrived the scheme and method of justification; it would have been a puzzling question to angels and men, had not he resolved it; *How should man*, sinful man, *be just with God?* But God, in his infinite wisdom, *found a ransom*, a Ransomer, a Redeemer of his people, to bring in everlasting righteousness for them, and thereby acquit and discharge them, and *deliver them from going down to the pit* of ruin and destruction; *God was in Christ reconciling the world to himself*; was, with him, forming the scheme of their peace and reconciliation, of their redemption, justification, and salvation; *not imputing their trespasses*, but the righteousness of his Son *unto them* (*Job 33:24; 2 Cor. 5:19*).

2. He sent his Son, in the fulness of time, to execute this scheme; he sent him in human nature, *made under the law*, subject to it, in the room and stead of his people, and to yield a perfect obedience to it; and he sent him *in the likeness of sinful flesh*, with their sins imputed to him; and by making him a sacrifice for sin, through his sufferings and death, he bore

the penalty of the law, that so the whole *righteousness of the law*, or all it could demand, both with respect to precept and penalty, *might be fulfilled in* them; they being represented by him (*Gal. 4:4; Rom. 8:3, 4*).

3. A perfect righteousness being wrought out by Christ, agreeable to the requirements of law and justice, by which the law is magnified and made honourable, and justice satisfied; God the Father approves of it, is well pleased with it, and accepts of it as the justifying righteousness of them that believe in Christ.

4. He imputes this righteousness to believers as their own: this is the Father's act of grace (*Rom. 4:6*). *Of Him*, that is, of God the Father, *are ye in Christ Jesus*, chosen in him, and united to him; *who, of God* (the Father) *is made unto us righteousness*; which is done by his act of imputation (*Rom. 4:6; 1 Cor 1:30*).

God the Son justifies

Secondly, God the Son, the second Person, is concerned in the justification of men; *By his knowledge*, says Jehovah the Father, *shall my righteous Servant justify many* (*Isa. 53:11*).

1. Christ, as a divine Person, as he has power to forgive sin, so to absolve and justify from it; of which we have some instances, even when he was here on earth, in human nature, as to the man sick of the palsy he said, *Thy sins are forgiven thee!* and to the woman taken in adultery, *Neither do I condemn thee!* which was a full acquittal and discharge; and to his apostles he

said, *Ye are clean*, every whit clean, free from sin, and fully absolved from it, *Through the word I have spoken to you*; the sentence of justification by his blood and righteousness he had pronounced upon them (*Matthew 9:2; John 8:11; 15:3; 13:10*).

2. As Mediator, Christ is the author of that righteousness by which sinners are justified; as he was to bring in an everlasting righteousness, he has brought in one; hence he is called, The Lord our Righteousness, the Sun of righteousness, and the end of the law for righteousness; and men are made righteous by his obedience, and justified by his blood (*Jer. 23:6; Mal. 4:2; Rom. 10:4; 5:9, 19*).

3. As the head and representative of his people, they are justified in him; as Adam's natural posterity, sinning in him, were condemned in him, judgment came upon them all unto condemnation; so all Christ's spiritual seed and offspring are justified in him; for *in the Lord shall all the seed of Israel be justified, and shall glory*; as he was *delivered* into the hands of justice and death *for their offences*, to make satisfaction for them, so he was *raised again for their justification*; and when he was raised, he was justified, acquitted, and discharged himself from all the sins of his people, imputed to him, having satisfied for them; and then they were justified in him (*Isa. 45:25; Rom. 4:25; 1 Tim. 3:16*).

4. As Christ has wrought out a righteousness for his people, so he actually puts it upon them, clothes them with it: says the church, *He hath covered me with the robe of righteousness*:

he is that Angel of the Lord before whom Joshua was brought, and accused by Satan; and to whom he himself said, *I will clothe thee with change of raiment* (*Isa. 61:10; Zech. 3:4*).

5. As it is to faith the righteousness of Christ is revealed, and by faith it is received, hence believers are said to be justified by faith; so this faith, as well as righteousness, is of Christ; as he is the object of it, *Ye believe in God, believe also in me*; so he is the *author* and *finisher* of it (*John 14:1; Heb. 12:2*).

God the Holy Spirit justifies

Thirdly, The Holy Spirit of God, the third Person, has also a concern in the justification of sinners.

1. He convinces men of righteousness, of their want of righteousness; of the weakness, imperfection, and insufficiency of their own righteousness, that they have none that can be called a righteousness; and that unless they have a better righteousness than that, they will never enter into the kingdom of heaven (*John 16:8*).

2. He brings near the righteousness of Christ; not only externally, in the ministry of the word; but internally, by the illumination of his grace; this is one of the things of Christ he takes and shows to souls enlightened by him; he shows them the fulness, glory, and suitableness of the righteousness of Christ, how perfect it is, how adequate to all the demands of law and justice, and how suitable to them; to cover their naked souls, to secure them from condemnation and death, to justify them

before God, and render them acceptable in his sight, and entitle them to eternal life.

3. He works faith in convinced and enlightened persons, to look at the righteousness of Christ, and take a view of its glories and excellencies; to approve of it, desire it, and to lay hold on it, and receive it as their justifying righteousness. Such a faith is of the operation of God, of the Spirit of God; it is what he works in the saints, and enables them to exercise it; hence he is called, *the Spirit of faith* (*Col.2:12; 2 Cor. 4:13*).

4. He bears witness to their spirits, that they are interested in the righteousness of Christ, and are justified by it; and he pronounces the sentence of justification in their consciences, or declares them justified, in the name of Christ, and on account of his righteousness; and which is the meaning of their being justified *in the name of the Lord Jesus, and by the Spirit of our God* (*1 Cor. 6:11*).

(3) WHO ARE THE OBJECTS OF JUSTIFICATION?

The objects of justification; and they are the elect. *Who shall lay anything to the charge of God's elect? It is God that justifieth!* that is, the elect (*Rom. 8:33*), for who else can be meant?

Elect men are justified

1. Elect men, and not elect angels; for though there are elect angels, and these are holy, just, and righteous; and so may be

declared to be what they are, just and righteous, and in that sense justified; yet, since they never laboured under the suspicion of a crime, nor were ever chargeable with any, they cannot, in a strict sense, be said to be justified. But elect men, who are sinners in Adam, as chosen in Christ their Head, are reckoned righteous; for justification is a branch of election, in which the elect are reckoned as righteous, through the righteousness of Christ; and these being the objects of justification, show the eternity of that act, since election was from the beginning, and before the foundation of the world; and the specialty of it, since the elect are a special and peculiar people; and the security of it, for it is certain, being closely connected with predestination, whom God predestinates, he calls and justifies; and its being a security from wrath and condemnation; for whom he justifies he glorifies (*Rom. 8:30*).

Redeemed persons are justified

2. Redeemed ones are the objects of justification; all that are chosen are redeemed; and all that are redeemed are justified; justification proceeds upon redemption; *Being justified freely by his grace, through the redemption that is in Christ Jesus* (*Rom. 3:24*), by which they are redeemed from all their iniquities, and from all the curses of the law due unto them, and so are acquitted and discharged.

3. Pardoned ones; for all that are chosen and redeemed are pardoned, and those are justified: the chosen are pardoned; for the Lord says, *I will pardon them whom I reserve* (*Jer. 50:20*), that is, whom he has reserved for himself by the act of election;

and the redeemed are pardoned; for forgiveness of sin is a branch of redemption; *In whom we have redemption, through his blood, the forgiveness of sin* (*Eph 1:7*), and whose sins are forgiven, they are justified (*Rom. 4:6, 7*).

Not all men justified

4. Hence it appears, that the objects of justification are not all men; for all men are not chosen; they are only a remnant, according to the election of grace: nor are all men redeemed; for those that are redeemed, are redeemed from among men, and out of every kindred, tongue, people, and nation: nor are all pardoned; for there are some whose sins go beforehand to judgment, and are never forgiven: nor do all men believe; faith is peculiar to God's elect: nor are all men saved from wrath, as they would be, if justified by the blood of Christ; some will go into everlasting punishment, when the righteous shall go into everlasting life: and so all are not justified; though there is an *all* that are justified, even all the seed and offspring of Christ, the seed of Israel, on whom the gift of righteousness comes to justification of life (*Isa. 45:25; Rom. 5:18*).

5. Yet they are many (*Isa. 53:11; Rom. 5:19*) for whom Christ gave his life a ransom; and whose blood was shed for the remission of their sins; those are said to be many (*Matthew 20:28; 26:28*).

Ungodly sinners are the objects of justification

6. The objects of justification are described as sinners, and ungodly; *sinners* (*Gal. 2:17*), *ungodly* (*Rom. 4:5*). So they are, in their unregenerate state: but when converted, they are

described as believers in Christ; for the righteousness of Christ is *unto all, and upon all them that believe*; it is applied unto them, and put upon them; and they have a comfortable sense and perception of their justification by it; they *believe in Jesus Christ, that they might be justified by the faith of Christ*; by Christ, the object of faith, and through believing in him, have a comfortable view of their justification before God, and acceptance with him; hence it is said, that *by him all that believe are justified*, openly and manifestly, and have the testimony and comfort of it within themselves; and these may be said to be *justified by faith*; by Christ, and his righteousness received by faith (*Rom. 5:1; 3:22; Gal. 2:16; Acts 13:39*), and such are not nominal believers, who only have a notional, historical faith, or who only profess to believe, as Simon Magus did; but who, *with the heart, believe unto righteousness*; who truly and heartily believe in the righteousness of Christ for their justification before God; and such shall never come into condemnation (*Rom. 10:10; John 5:24*).

(4) WHAT THE ELECT ARE JUSTIFIED FROM

The charges, or sins, such are justified from. *Who shall lay any thing to the charge of God's elect? It is God that justifieth* (*Rom. 8:33*) from all charges, all that may be truly brought against them, all criminal charges they are chargeable with.

Justified from original sin

1. They are chargeable with original sin, the sin of the first man; they were, seminally, in his loins, when he ate the forbidden

[55]

fruit; as Levi was in the loins of Abraham, when he paid tithes to Melchizedek: they were federally in him, as their covenant head and representative, and sinning in him, they became chargeable therewith; and judgment so far proceeded against them, as to bring them under the sentence of condemnation and death; but God justifies and acquits them from that offence, through the gift of his Son's righteousness, which comes unto them to justification of life; and he frees them from the charge of that disobedience by which they were made sinners, through the imputation of Christ's obedience to them (*Rom. 5:12, 18, 19*).

Justified from impurity of nature

2. They are chargeable with impurity of nature, and a want of original righteousness; which Adam, by sinning, lost, and all his posterity are without it; they are conceived in sin, and bring an impure nature into the world with them; which is the case of all, even of God's elect. The law requires purity and holiness of nature, and charges with the want of it; but God justifies from this charge, through the imputation of the holiness of Christ's human nature to them, which is a branch of their justification; and is thought, by some divines, to be *the law of the Spirit of life* in him, which *frees from the law of sin and death*; and who is made, to his people, *sanctification* and righteousness; and was typified by the high priest, having an inscription on his forehead, *Holiness to the Lord* (*Rom. 8:2; 1 Cor. 1:30; Ex. 28:36*).

Justified from sins before conversion

3. They are chargeable with actual sins, before conversion,

and those many, and some very heinous; and yet God justifies from them all; as Saul was chargeable with blasphemy, persecution, and doing injury to others; but obtained pardoning mercy, and a justifying righteousness: the Corinthians were guilty of some of the blackest crimes, and most enormous sins, yet were justified, in the name of the Lord Jesus, and by the Spirit of our God: the apostles, and others, before conversion, were disobedient, serving divers lusts and pleasures; and yet were justified, by the grace of God, and made heirs, according to the hope of eternal life (*1 Tim. 1:13; 1 Cor. 6:9-11; Titus 3:3, 7*).

Justified from sins after conversion

4. They are chargeable with a multitude of sins, after conversion; with many revoltings, and sometimes with great backslidings; their failings and infirmities, errors and mistakes, are innumerable; yet all are forgiven, and they are cleansed and justified from them (*Jas. 3:2; Ps. 19:12; Hosea 14:4*).

5. They are justified from all their sins, of whatsoever kind, that they can be charged with; for they that believe in Christ, *are justified from all things*, from all sins, from all criminal charges; God forgives all their trespasses, for Christ's sake, and his blood cleanses from all sin (*Acts 13:39; Col. 2:13; 1 John 1:7*).

6. They are justified by the righteousness of Christ, *from all things, from which they could not be justified by the law of Moses*; for there were some sins which the law made no provision of sacrifice for, as adultery and murder; such therefore that *despised Moses' law*, by breaking it in such

instances, *died without mercy*; but God justifies from all such sins, as well as others, through the righteousness of Christ (*Acts 13:39; Heb. 10:28; 9:15, 26*).

Justified from all charges, whether true or false

7. God justifies his elect from all charges brought against them, from what quarter soever, and whether true or false; do they bring charges against themselves, as they often do? conscience, which is as a thousand witnesses, accuses and condemns them; but though their hearts and consciences condemn them, God is greater than their hearts, and knows all things; what provisions he has made for them in covenant, what a righteousness his Son has wrought out for their justification; and though as on one hand, if a good man knows nothing by himself, yet he is not hereby justified; so on the other, though he knows much by himself and against himself, yet God clears him from all. Do saints bring charges one against another, sometimes rightly, and sometimes wrongly, whether privately or publicly: and do not forgive one another, as they should do, since God, for Christ's sake, forgives them? yet God forgives all, and clears from all charges, true or false. Does the world bring charges against them, as they frequently do, even speak all manner of evil of them falsely, for Christ's sake, as Tertullus the orator, against the apostle Paul? yet every tongue that riseth up in judgment against them God will condemn; for their *righteousness is of me, saith the Lord*; plainly suggesting, that he would justify and acquit them from all (*Isa. 54:17*). Does Satan go about the earth to pick up charges against the people of God, and then accuse them to him, as he did Job, whence he is called,

the accuser of the brethren? Jehovah repels his charges, and rebukes him for them; an instance of this we have in the vision of Zechariah (*Zech. 3:1-4*). In a word, whatever charges the law of God brings against the elect, which is broken by them, and for which it accuses, pronounces guilty, curses and condemns, and whatever charges the justice of God can produce against them, the mouth of the one, and of the other, is stopped by the righteousness of Christ; by which the one is honoured and magnified; and the other is satisfied and well pleased; and so a full justification from all charges takes place, and God is just while he is the justifier of him that believes in Jesus.

(5) THE MATTER AND MANNER OF JUSTIFICATION

The matter and form of justification, the righteousness of Christ imputed: the matter of justification, or that for the sake of which a sinner is justified, is the righteousness of Christ; the form and manner in which it is made over to such an one, and becomes his, is by imputation.

(5A) THE MATTER OF JUSTIFICATION

First, The matter of justification, the righteousness of Christ; and everything else must be removed from it, and denied of it. As,

A man cannot be justified by his own righteousness

1*st*, a man's own righteousness, or his obedience to the law; this is expressly denied to be that by which a sinner can be justified; *By the deeds of the law, there shall no flesh be justified in his sight*, in the sight of God; that is, by works done in obedience to the law; and which is meant, not of the ceremonial, but the moral law; that law by which is the knowledge of sin, and which pronounces a man guilty of it before God, and stops his mouth, as the context shows; and is opposed to grace, which the ceremonial law is not, being of grace, given to relieve, under a sense of sin, by pointing to the Saviour, and his propitiatory sacrifice; and hence this conclusion is drawn, *Therefore we conclude, that a man is justified by faith*; by Christ and his righteousness, the object of faith; *without the works of the law* being joined to Christ, and his righteousness, or considered as any part of a justifying righteousness (*Rom. 3:20, 28*). And to the same purpose are the words of the apostle, in Galatians 2:16.

The reasons why a man's own righteousness cannot be the matter of his justification before God, are,

1. Because it is imperfect, and the law will not admit of an imperfect righteousness for justification; it requires perfect, sinless obedience; and not anything short of that will it allow to be a righteousness; *It shall be our righteousness*, says Moses, *if we observe to do all these commandments, before the Lord our God, as he hath commanded us* (*Deut. 6:25*), so that if there is any failure, either in the matter or manner of obedience, it is no righteousness; and such obedience and righteousness, men, since the fall, were never capable of; the people of Israel, in general, followed after the law of righteousness; but did not attain to it, seeking it not by faith in

Christ, in whom it is only found; but, as it were, by the works of the law, in which there is a deficiency, and so no righteousness: and those among them who made the largest pretensions to righteousness, fell short of it, as the Scribes and Pharisees; insomuch, that if a man's righteousness does not exceed theirs, he cannot enter into the kingdom of heaven; nay, even the works of the truly just and good, are not perfect; *There is not a just man upon earth, that doeth good and sinneth not* (*Eccl. 7:20*), hence good men, sensible of the insufficiency of their own righteousness, decline and deprecate entering into judgment with God upon that foot, acknowledging the impurity and imperfection of their obedience; on account of which, they know they could not be just with God (*Job 9:2, 3, 20, 32; Ps. 143:2; Isa. 64:6*).

2. If justification was by the works of men, it could not be by grace; for grace and works are opposed, and cannot consist together in the business of justification; for if it is of grace, then not of works; but justification is by grace, and therefore not by works; *Being justified freely by his grace* (*Rom. 3:24*), not only by grace, but freely by it; or by grace that is altogether free; and, indeed, as Austin says, it would not be grace if it was not so, or was any ways clogged with the works of men.

3. If justification was by man's obedience, it would not be by a righteousness without works, and that imputed, as it is; if it is by a man's own righteousness, then not by a righteousness without works, for that consists entirely of works; and if a man's own, then not imputed; whereas, the blessedness of

justification, lies in the imputation of a righteousness without works (*Rom. 4:6*).

4. If justification could be by men's obedience to the law, then there would have been no need of the righteousness of Christ, nor of his coming into the world to work out one; it would have been an unnecessary thing for God to send his Son, that the righteousness of the law might be fulfilled in us, by him, if we could have fulfilled it ourselves; and not only his life, and the obedience of it, would have been useless, but his death also; for, as the apostle argues, *If righteousness came by the law, then Christ is dead in vain* (*Gal. 2:21*).

5. If justification was by the works of men, boasting would be encouraged; whereas, God's design in the whole scheme of salvation, and so in this branch of it, is to prevent it, lest any man should boast; *Where is boasting then? It is excluded. By what law? of works? Nay, but by the law of faith*; that is, not by the doctrine of justification, by the works of men, that would establish boasting; but by the doctrine of justification by faith in the righteousness of Christ, which leaves no room for it (*Rom. 3:27*).

A man not justified by his obedience to the gospel

2ndly, Nor is man's obedience to the gospel, as to a new and milder law, the matter of his justification before God. It was a notion, that some years ago obtained, that a relaxation of the law, and the severity of it, has been obtained by Christ; and a new law, a remedial law, a law of milder terms, has been introduced by him, which is the gospel; the terms of which are, faith, repentance, and new obedience; and though these are imperfect, yet being sincere, they are accepted of by God, in the room of a perfect righteousness. But every article of this scheme is wrong; for,

1. The law is not relaxed, nor any of its severity abated; there is no alteration made in it; neither with respect to its precepts, nor its penalty; it requires the same holy, just, and good things, it ever did; Christ came not to destroy it, but to fulfil it: nor is the sanction of it removed; though it is not made for, or does not lie against, a righteous man; yet it is made for, and lies against, the sinner and transgressor; and as it has the same commanding, so the same condemning power, to them that are under it; it accuses, pronounces guilty, condemns, and curses, even such who continue not in all things to observe it.

2. Nor is the gospel a new law; there is nothing in it that looks like a law; it has no commands in it, but all promises; it is a pure declaration of grace and salvation by Christ; therefore called, the gospel of the grace of God, and the gospel of our salvation.

3. Nor are faith, repentance, and new obedience, the terms of it, and required by it, as conditions of men's acceptance with God; faith and repentance, as doctrines, are gospel doctrines, and parts of the gospel ministry; and as graces, are not terms and conditions required in it, to be performed by men of themselves; they are blessings of grace, declared in it, and are

gifts of grace bestowed on men; faith is the gift of God, and repentance is a grant from him; and both they, and new and spiritual obedience, are provided for in the covenant of grace (*Ezek. 36:26, 27*).

4. If these were terms and conditions, required of men, in the gospel, to be performed by them, in order to their acceptance with God, the gospel would not be a remedial law; nor these milder terms than those of the old law; for it was easier for Adam, in a state of innocence, to have kept the whole law, than it is for man, in his fallen state, to repent and believe in Christ, and perform new and spiritual obedience of himself; till God takes away the stony heart, and gives an heart of flesh, and gives grace, as well as time and space, to repent, men never will nor can repent of their sins: and faith is not of a man's self; no man can come to Christ, that is, believe in him, unless it be given to him, and the Father draws him; and without Christ, his Spirit and grace, a man cannot do any good thing.

5. Nor is it true, that God will accept of an imperfect righteousness in the room of a perfect one: nor can anything more highly reflect upon the justice and truth of God, who is the Judge of all the earth, and will do right, and whose judgment is according to truth, and can never account that a righteousness which is not one.

A profession of religion not the matter of justification
3rdly, nor is a profession of religion, even of the best religion,

[64]

the Christian religion, the matter of justification before God; men may have a form of godliness without the power of it; they may submit to the ordinances of Christ, baptism, and the Lord's Supper, and attend every duty of religion, and yet be far from righteousness: and even if a profession of religion was taken up upon right principles, on a good foundation, and held and maintained in an honourable manner, and even though a man may be ever so sincere in it, it is not the matter of his justification. For,

Sincerity in true religion is not the matter of justification

4thly, sincerity itself, in any religion, even in the best religion, is not a justifying righteousness. There may be sincerity in a bad religion, as well as in a good one; a man may be sincerely wrong, as well as sincerely right; may be a sincere Pagan, a sincere Papist, and a sincere Mohammedan, as well as a sincere Christian; yea, a man may be a sincere blasphemer of Christ, and a sincere persecutor of his followers, as the apostle Paul was, before conversion, and as the persecutors of Christ's disciples (*Acts 26:9; John 16:2*), and taking sincerity in the best sense, as a grace of the Spirit of God, which accompanies all other graces, and denominates faith unfeigned, hope without hypocrisy, and love without dissimulation; it belongs to sanctification, and not justification; and is not the whole, nor any part of justifying righteousness.

The act of believing is not the matter of justification

5thly, nor faith, the act of believing; this is, by some, said to be imputed for righteousness; but is not so; for,

[65]

1. Faith, as a man's act, is his own; and is called *his* faith, *thy* faith, and *my* faith (*Hab. 2:4; Matthew 9:22; 15:28; Jas. 2:18*), whereas, the righteousness by which a man is justified, is not his own, but another's, and therefore not faith.

2. Faith is imperfect; it is so in the greatest believers; the disciples of Christ saw need to pray, Lord, *increase our faith!* whereas, a righteousness to justify must be perfect; nothing else can be accounted a righteousness.

3. Faith is not everlasting; as to its use; is only for the present life; it will be changed into vision: but the righteousness by which sinners are justified before God, and which was brought in by Christ for that purpose, is *everlasting righteousness* (*Dan. 9:24*).

4. Faith and righteousness are manifestly distinguished; *The righteousness of God is revealed from faith to faith*; and therefore faith cannot be that righteousness. *With the heart man believeth unto righteousness*; and therefore righteousness must be a distinct thing from faith; which *righteousness is unto all, and upon all them that believe*; and therefore must be different from that faith with which they believe (*Rom. 1:17; 10:10; 3:22*).

5. Something else, and not faith, is said to be that by which men are made righteous, and justified; as *the obedience of one*, Jesus Christ, by which *many are made righteous*; and the blood of Christ; *being justified by his blood* (*Rom. 5:9, 19*). Now

faith is neither the one nor the other; and though men are said to be *justified by faith (Rom. 5:1)*, yet not as an act of men; for then they would be justified by works, contrary to express scripture; nor by it as a grace of the Spirit in men; for this would confound justification and sanctification together; but by the object of it, Christ, and his righteousness, apprehended, received, and embraced by faith. And though believers are said to be justified by faith, yet faith is never said to justify them.

6. The passages produced to establish this notion, that faith is a man's righteousness, are insufficient; *Abraham believed God, and it was counted to him for righteousness (Rom. 4:3)*. And again (*Rom. 4:5*), *His faith is counted for righteousness*. And in (*Rom. 4:9*), *We say, that faith was reckoned to Abraham for righteousness*. Now this cannot be understood of the act of Abraham's faith; but of the object of it, or that which he believed in, the righteousness of Christ, which God imputes, without works (*Rom. 4:6*), and that this must be the sense is clear, from this one single consideration, that the same *it* which was imputed to Abraham for righteousness, is imputed to all those who believe in God, who raised up Christ from the dead (*Rom. 4:22-24*). Now supposing Abraham's faith was imputed to him for a justifying righteousness; it cannot reasonably be thought that it should be imputed also for righteousness to all that believe in all succeeding ages.

Sanctification is not the matter of justification

6thly, Nor is the whole of sanctification the matter of justification; these two are distinct things, and not to be confounded; the one is a work of grace within men, the other an act of God's grace towards and upon men; the one is imperfect, the other perfect; the one is carried on gradually, the other done at once.

THE SOLE MATTER OF JUSTIFICATION

But the sole matter of justification, or that for the sake of which a sinner is justified before God, is the righteousness of Christ; and which is,

1. Not his essential righteousness, as God; the righteousness by which men are justified is the righteousness of God, which was wrought out by Christ, who is God as well as man; but it is not that righteousness which is essential to him as God; he that is their righteousness is Jehovah, but the righteousness by which he is Jehovah, or which belongs to him as such, is not their righteousness, as Osiander dreamed; for this would be to deify them.

2. Nor his righteousness, integrity, and fidelity, which he exercised in the discharge of his mediatorial office; that was personal and respected himself, and not relative to others; he was faithful to him that appointed him to that office, and he did his work in so upright a manner, that he obtained the character of God's *righteous servant* (*Isa. 11:5; 53:11*), but though it is a righteousness he wrought out as mediator, which is imputed for justification, yet it is not his mediatorial righteousness, or the righteousness of

his office, or that by which he showed the discharge of it.

3. Nor does it consist of all the actions and works he did here on earth, nor of what he is doing in heaven; it wholly consists of those he wrought in his state of humiliation here on earth, yet not all of these; not his extraordinary and miraculous works, these were proofs of his Deity, and of his Messiahship; they were done and recorded to engage men to believe in him, and in his righteousness; but were no ingredients, as one observes, in that righteousness on which they were to believe. Nor is his work in heaven, appearing for his people there, interceding for them, and preparing mansions of glory for them, any part of the righteousness wrought out for them, and imputed to them. But [the sole matter of justification is],

4. What he did and suffered in their nature on earth, and in their room and stead, and as their substitute and representative, commonly called his active and passive obedience; to which may be added the purity and holiness of his nature, and which altogether made up *the righteousness of the law* which was *fulfilled* by him, as their head and representative (*Rom. 8:4*), for whatever the law required is necessary to a sinner's justification before God; and that requires of sinners more than it did of man in innocence. Man was created with a pure and holy nature, conformable to the pure and holy law of God; and it was incumbent on him to continue so, and to yield in it perfect and sinless obedience; and in failure thereof he was threatened with death; and now having sinned, whereby his nature is vitiated and corrupted, and his obedience

become faulty and imperfect, suffering the penalty of the law is required; and all this is requisite to the justification of a sinner, purity of nature, perfection of obedience, and sufferings of death; all which meet in Christ, the representative of his people, in whom they are justified.

Christ's holy nature requisite to justification

Firstly. Holiness of nature: some consider this only as a qualification for his office, and the due performance of it in human nature; whereby he was capable of yielding sinless obedience to the law, and was qualified as an high priest to offer himself a spotless sacrifice, and to be a proper advocate for sinners, being Jesus Christ the righteous; but this not only fitted him for his work, but made him suitable to us, *Such an high priest became us, who is holy, harmless*; the law required an holy nature in conformity to it; it is wanting in us, it is found in Christ, *who is of God made to us sanctification.*

Christ's obedience justifies

Secondly. The obedience of Christ's life, commonly called his active obedience, which was sinless and perfect; his whole life was in perfect conformity to the law, and was a continued series of holiness and obedience; the holiness of his nature appeared in all his actions, throughout his whole state of humiliation, from his birth to his death; in all which he was the representative of his people; what he did, he did in their room and stead, and therefore was reckoned as if done by them, and is imputed to them as their righteousness: there are some divines who exclude the active obedience of Christ from being any part of the righteousness by which men are justified; they allow it is a condition requisite in him as mediator, qualifying him for his office; but deny that it is the matter of justification, or that it is imputed and reckoned for righteousness to men. They suppose that Christ was obliged to this obedience for himself as a creature, and that it is unnecessary to his people, because his sufferings and death are sufficient for their justification. But,

1. Though the human nature of Christ being a creature, and so considered, was subject to a law and obliged to obedience; yet it was not obliged to a course of obedience in such a low, mean, and suffering state, being entitled to glory and happiness from the moment of its union to the Son of God; this was voluntary: besides, the human nature being taken into personal union with the Son of God, the person of Christ, who was not subject to the law, but was above it, and Lord of it; it was an act of his will to submit to it, and a wonderful instance of his condescension it was; moreover, as Christ being made of a woman, and was made under the law, he was made both for the sake of his people; he became man for their sake, *to us or for us a child is born* (*Isa. 9:6*), and for their sake he became subject to the law, that he might yield obedience to it in their room and stead, and that he might redeem them from the curse of it; and this was the kind and gracious design of his divine Father in sending him in the likeness of sinful flesh, that he might both obey and suffer for them, that so the whole righteousness of the law might be fulfilled in them (*Gal. 4:4; Rom. 8:3, 4*).

2. Without the active obedience of Christ the law would not be satisfied, the language of which is *Do and live (Lev. 18:5; Ezek. 20:11; Rom. 10:5)* and unless its precepts are obeyed, as well as its penalty endured, it cannot be satisfied; and unless it is satisfied, there can be no justification by it; Christ, as a surety, in the room and stead of his people, must both obey the precepts of the law and bear its penalty; his submitting to the one, without conforming to the other, is not sufficient; one debt is not paid by another; his paying off the debt of punishment did not exempt from obedience, as the paying off the debt of obedience did not exempt from punishment: Christ did not satisfy the whole law by either of them separately, but by both conjunctly; by his sufferings and death he satisfied the threatenings, the sanction of the law, but not the precepts of it thereby; and by his active obedience he satisfied the preceptive part of the law, but not the penal part; but by both, he satisfied the whole of the law and made it honourable.

3. It is by a righteousness that men are justified, and that is the righteousness of Christ; now righteousness, strictly speaking lies in doing, in actual obedience to the commands of the law, *This shall be our righteousness, if we observe to do*, &c. (*Deut. 6:25*). Christ's righteousness lay in doing, not in suffering; "all righteousness," as one says, "is either an habit or an act; but sufferings are neither, and therefore not righteousness; no man is righteous because he is punished; if so, the devils and damned in hell would be righteous in proportion to their punishment; the more severe their punishment, and the more grievous their torments, the

greater their righteousness must be; if there is any righteousness in punishment, it must be in the punisher, and not in the punished."

If therefore men are justified by the righteousness of Christ imputed to them, it must be by his active obedience, and not merely by his sufferings and death; because these, though they free from death, yet, strictly speaking, do not make men righteous.

4. It is expressly said, that *by the obedience of one shall many be made righteous (Rom. 5:19)*, which cannot be meant of the sufferings and death of Christ; because, properly speaking, they are not his obedience, but the effect of it; besides, the antithesis in the text determines the sense of the words; for if by one man's actual disobedience, which was the case, many were made sinners, so by the rule of opposition, by one man's actual obedience, which is Christ's, many are made righteous, or justified.

5. The reward of life is not promised to suffering, but to doing; the law says, *Do this and live (Lev. 18:5; Ezek. 20:11; Rom. 10:5; Gal. 3:12)* ; it promises life, not to him that suffers the penalty, but to him that obeys the precept; "there never was a law," as an excellent divine observes [Goodwin], "even among men, either promising or declaring a reward due to the criminal, because he had undergone the punishment of his crimes."

Christ's sufferings and death being satisfactory to the comminatory [a formal denunciation] or threatening part of the law, are reckoned to us for justification, that so we may be freed and discharged from the curse of it, and from hell and wrath to come; but as they do not constitute us righteous, they do not entitle us to eternal life; but the active obedience or righteousness of Christ being imputed to us, is *unto justification of life (Rom. 5:18)*, or is what gives the title to eternal life.

Christ's sufferings and death requisite to justification

Thirdly. Nevertheless the sufferings and death of Christ, or what is commonly called his passive obedience, are requisite to our justification before God. Passive obedience is a phrase that may be objected to as not accurate, being a seeming contradiction in terms; suffering and obedience convey different ideas, and belong to different classes; suffering belongs to the predicament or class of passion, obedience to that of action; yet as Christ's sufferings flow from his obedience, and were the effect of his submission to his Father's will, with respect to which he said, *Not my will but thine be done*; and as he was obedient throughout his life, in all the actions and in all the sufferings of it, even to the moment of his death; and was also obedient in death, laying down his life at the command received from his Father; *For though a Son, yet learned he obedience by the things he suffered*; and was even active in his sufferings; he laid down his life of himself, he poured out his soul unto death, and gave himself an offering, and a sacrifice for sin; considering these things, the phrase, passive obedience, may be admitted of; especially as it is well known what is meant by it, the voluntary sufferings and death of Christ, which are most certainly ingredients in the justification of a sinner *(Luke 22:42; Heb. 5:8)*.

If Christ's righteousness justifies, why did he have to die?

It may be asked, if Christ was the representative of his people in his active obedience, which constitutes them just or righteous, and is their justification of life, or what entitles to eternal life, what need was there of his sufferings and death? to which it may be answered, that it was necessary that Christ, as the surety and representative of his people, should satisfy the law in everything it could require of them, both as creatures, and as sinful creatures. As creatures, the law could require of them purity of nature, and perfect obedience to it, which were in their first parents, but were lost by them, and are wanting in them; as sinful creatures, it could require of them to endure the penalty of it. Christ now as the surety of his people, represented them as creatures, in the purity of his nature and in the perfection of his life, or in his active obedience; and presented that to the law for them which it could require of them as creatures: and as it is certain he represented them in his sufferings and death, hence he is said to die for them, that is, in their room and stead, and they to be crucified and buried with him; in these he represented them as sinful creatures, and bore the penalty or curse of the law; and in both obediences he satisfied the whole of it; and as by the one they are freed from death the sanction of the law, so by the other they are entitled to life, and by both Christ is the fulfilling end of the law for righteousness unto them. For that the sufferings and death of Christ, as well as his active obedience, are requisite to the complete justification of a sinner, appears,

1. That without these the law would not be satisfied, and all its demands answered; and unless it is satisfied; there can be no

justification by it; and it cannot be satisfied unless its penalty is endured; for,

2. The law, in case of disobedience to it, threatened with death, and death is the just wages and due demerit of sin; and therefore this must be endured, either by the sinner or a surety for him, or else he cannot be discharged by the law.

3. The justification of a sinner is expressly ascribed to the blood of Christ, which is put for the whole of his sufferings and death (*Rom. 5:9*).

4. Justification proceeds upon redemption, *being justified freely by his grace, through the redemption that is in Christ Jesus* (*Rom. 3:24*) now redemption is by the blood of Christ, and through his sufferings and death (*Eph. 1:7; 1 Pet. 3:18, 19; Rev. 5:9*).

5. It is upon the foot of Christ's satisfaction that justification takes place, and satisfaction is made by Christ's doing and suffering all the law requires; and so as by his obedience, likewise by his blood and death, to which it is more frequently ascribed, peace is made by his blood, reconciliation by his death, atonement and expiation by his sacrifice, which is of a sweet smelling savour to God (*Col. 1:20; Rom. 5:10; Heb. 9:26; Eph. 5:2*).

6. The complete justification of a sinner, does not seem to be finished by Christ until his resurrection, after his obedience

and sufferings of death; for he *was delivered for our offences, and was raised again for our justification* (*Rom. 4:25*). In short, the righteousness by which we are justified, as Dr. Ames says, is not to be sought for in different operations of Christ, but arises from his whole obedience, both active and passive; which is both satisfactory and meritorious, and frees from condemnation and death, and adjudges and entitles to eternal life; even as one and the same disobedience of Adam, stripped us of original righteousness, and rendered us obnoxious to condemnation. So much for the matter of justification.

(5B) THE MANNER OF JUSTIFICATION - IMPUTATION

Secondly, The form of it, is imputation; or the manner in which the righteousness of Christ is made over to a sinner, and it becomes his, is by imputing it to him; *Even as David describeth the blessedness of the man unto whom God imputeth righteousness without works* (*Rom. 4:6*). The words used both in Hebrew and Greek, signify, to reckon, repute, estimate, attribute, and place something to the account of another: as when the apostle said to Philemon, concerning Onesimus, *If he hath wronged thee, or oweth thee ought, put that on my account*, let it be reckoned, or imputed to me. So when God is said to impute the righteousness of Christ to any, the sense is, that he reckons it as theirs, being wrought out for them, and accounts them righteous by it, as though they had performed it in their own persons: and that it is by the righteousness of Christ, imputed to his people, that they are justified, is clear, when it is observed,

1. That those whom God justifies, are, in themselves, ungodly; for God *justifieth the ungodly* (Rom. 4:5), if ungodly, then without a righteousness; and if without a righteousness, then, if they are justified, it must be by a righteousness imputed to them, or placed to their account; which can be no other than the righteousness of Christ.

2. They that are justified, are justified either by an inherent, or by an imputed righteousness: not by an inherent one, for that is imperfect, and so not justifying; and if not by an inherent righteousness, then it must be by one imputed to them, for there remains no other.

3. The righteousness by which any are justified, is the righteousness of another, and not their own, even the righteousness of Christ; *Not having on mine own righteousness*, says the apostle (*Phil. 3:9*). Now the righteousness of another, cannot be made a man's, or he be justified by it, any other way than by an imputation of it to him.

4. The same way that Adam's sin, became the sin of his posterity, or they were made sinners by it, the same way Christ's righteousness becomes his people's, or they are made righteous by it. Now the former is by imputation; and so the latter; *As by one man's disobedience many were made sinners*; that is, by the imputation of it to them; *so by the obedience of one*

shall many be made righteous; that is, by placing it to their account (*Rom. 5:19*).

5. The same way that the sins of Christ's people became his, his righteousness becomes theirs. Now their sins became Christ's by imputation only; the Father laid them on him, or made them to meet upon him, imputed them to him, placed them to his account; and he took them upon him, and looked upon himself as answerable to justice for them; and so, in the same way, his righteousness is made over to, and put upon his people; *For he who knew no sin, was made sin for us*, by imputation, *that we might be made the righteousness of God in him*; accounted righteous in him, through his righteousness imputed (*2 Cor. 5:21*).

The excellency of Christ's righteousness

Now there are several things which are said of this imputed righteousness of Christ, which serve greatly to recommend it, and set forth the excellency of it; as,

1. That it is called *the righteousness of God* (*Rom. 1:17; 3:22*), being wrought by Christ, who is God as well as man; approved and accepted of by God, and freely imputed by him to believers, as their justifying righteousness.

2. It is called, *the righteousness of One* (*Rom. 5:18*), of one of the Persons in the Trinity, the Son of God; of him, who, though he has two natures united in him, is but one Person, and who is the one common Head to all his seed; and though his

obedience, or righteousness, serves for many, it is *the obedience of One* (*Rom. 5:19*), and therefore they are justified, not partly by their own obedience, and partly by Christ's, but by his only.

3. It is called, *the righteousness of the law* (*Rom. 8:4*), being wrought by Christ in conformity to the law; so that this righteousness is a legal righteousness, as performed by Christ, being every way commensurate to the demands of it; though evangelical, as made over to his people, and revealed in the gospel; for it is manifested without the law, though witnessed to by law and prophets.

4. It is called, *the righteousness of faith* (*Rom. 4:13*), not that faith is righteousness, or imputed for it, or is the matter of a justifying righteousness, or any part of it; but because the righteousness of Christ is revealed to faith, and that lays hold on it, receives it, rejoices in it, and boasts of it.

5. It is called, *the gift of righteousness*, and *the free gift*, and *the gift by grace* (*Rom. 5:15-17*), because freely wrought out by Christ, and freely imputed by God the Father; and faith is freely given to receive and embrace it.

6. It is called, *a robe of righteousness*, a garment down to the feet, which covers the whole mystical body of Christ (*Isa. 61:10; Rev. 1:13*), it is signified by *gold of Ophir*, *clothing of wrought gold*, and *raiment of needle work*; setting forth the preciousness of it (*Ps. 45:9,13,14*). It is said to be *change of raiment*, and the *wedding garment*

(*Zech. 3:4; Matthew 22:12*), yea, the*best robe* (*uke 15:22*), a better robe than Adam had in Eden, or the angels in heaven; theirs, at best, being but the righteousness of a creature, and hat loseable, as the event showed; but Christ's righteousness is the righteousness of God, and an everlasting one; it may be rendered, the *first robe*, being first in designation, and in the provision of the covenant of grace; though Adam's robe of righteousness was first in wear and use.

(6) THE EFFECTS OF JUSTIFICATION

The effects of justification by the righteousness of Christ may be next considered, which are as follows.

Freedom from all penal evils

1. An entire freedom from all penal evils, in this life and in that which is to come. Justified ones are not freed from all evils; they have their evil things now, as Lazarus had, but they are not brought upon them by way of punishment; afflictions are evils in themselves, being not joyous but grievous; but then they are not penal ones; they are fatherly chastisements, they are fruits and evidences of the love of God to them, and not of his vindictive wrath (*Rev. 3:19; 1 Cor. 11:32*); death was threatened as a punishment for sin, and is the just demerit of it, and as such is inflicted on unrighteous ones, but is no penal evil to justified ones; it is their privilege and not their punishment (*1 Cor. 3:22; Rev. 14:13*), and therefore their death is desirable, even by wicked men, as it was by Balaam: nor will any penal evil befall the justified ones after death; for *being*

now justified by his (Christ's) *blood*, they *shall be saved from wrath through him (Rom. 5:9)*; from wrath to come, the vengeance of eternal fire: should any penal evil be inflicted on them here or hereafter, it would highly reflect upon the justice of God, in punishing twice for the same offences, once in their surety, and again in themselves, since the chastisement, or punishment of their sins has been laid on Christ, and he has endured it; and therefore it would be a lessening of the value of Christ's satisfaction, as if it was not made to full content, should punishment be inflicted in any degree upon those for whom it is made; and it would be contrary to the gospel declaration, that they that believe in Christ are justified, and shall not enter into condemnation.

Peace with God

2. Peace with God is another fruit and effect of justification; being *justified by faith, we have peace with God* (*Rom. 5:1*), peace with God is made by the blood of Christ, and reconciliation by his death; and besides that, there is a peace of conscience which is had in a way of believing, and through a comfortable sense and perception of an interest in the righteousness of Christ, the effect of which is peace and quietness (*Isa. 32:17*).

Access to God

3. Access to God through Christ; for having a comfortable view by faith of interest in the righteousness of Christ unto justification, it follows, *by whom also we have access by faith into this grace wherein we stand* (*Rom. 5:2*), access to God

as the God of grace, to him as on a throne of grace, to all the blessings of grace which come from God through Christ; and through the blood and righteousness of Christ justified ones have great freedom, boldness and confidence, to go to God, and present their supplication to him for what they want; not for their righteousness' sake, but in their requests making mention of the righteousness of Christ, and only pleading the worth and virtue of that.

Acceptance with God

4. Acceptance with God through Christ follows upon justification by his righteousness; there can be no acceptance with God upon the foot of a man's own righteousness, which cannot render him acceptable to God; but through the righteousness of Christ there is an acceptance both of persons and services; first of persons and then of services; as God had respect to Abel, and so to his offering, and accepted it; so he has respect to the persons of his justified ones, as considered in Christ; he has respect to him, and is well pleased with him, and with all that are in him; they are accepted of God in the beloved, being clothed with the robe of his righteousness, and the garments of his salvation; and their services being done in the strength of Christ, and through faith in him, and to the glory of God by him, and their spiritual sacrifices being offered up by him their great high-priest, they become acceptable to God through him.

Present and future well-being

5. The well-being of God's people here and hereafter depends upon their justification, and is a consequent of it; *Say ye to the*

righteous, one that is justified by the righteousness of Christ, *that it shall be well with him* (*Isa. 3:10*), it is well with the justified ones in life; be it with them as it may, all is well with them and for the best; all things work together for their good, adversity and prosperity; what they have of worldly things, though but little (*Ps. 37:16; Prov. 15:16, 17*), are blessings to them: it is well with such an one at death, he has hope in it, and rejoices in hope of the glory of God; peace is the end of the perfect and upright man, who is perfectly righteous through the righteousness of Christ imputed to him; and it is well with him at judgment, he has a righteousness that will answer for him in that time to come; and he shall have an abundant entrance into the everlasting kingdom and glory of our Lord Jesus Christ; and it will be well with him to all eternity; he that is righteous will then be righteous still, and ever continue so, and shall go into everlasting life.

Glorying in Christ

6. Glorying, or boasting, is another effect of justification; not in a man's self, in his own righteousness; not of his duties, services, and performance; nor of blessings of goodness enjoyed through his own merit; nor of heaven and happiness, as his own acquisition; all such boasting is excluded, by the doctrine of justification by faith in the righteousness of Christ; but such as are justified in Christ, glory of him, in whom they are justified; and glory in this, that he is *of God, made to them righteousness* (*Isa. 45:25; 1 Cor. 1:30*).

Eternal life and certainty of salvation

7. Justified ones have an undoubted title to eternal life; hence

justification by Christ's righteousness is called, *justification of life*, because it entitles to it; and such are *made heirs, according to the hope of eternal life*; are heirs of the inheritance, incorruptible and undefiled, and reserved in the heavens, and shall be possessed of it (*Rom. 5:18; Titus 3:7*). For,

8. Certainty of salvation may be concluded from justification; such as are justified, shall most assuredly be *saved from wrath*; there is an inseparable connection between justification and glorification; *Whom he justified, them he also glorified* (*Rom. 5:9; 8:30*).

(7) THE PROPERTIES OF JUSTIFICATION

An act of God's grace

1. It is an act of God's grace, of pure grace, without any consideration of merit, worthiness, and works of men; grace is the moving cause of it, as has been already observed; it was according to the purpose and grace of God, that he resolved upon the justification of any of the sons of men; *The scripture foreseeing that God would justify the heathen through faith* (*Gal. 3:8*), the scripture foresaw, or predicted, the justification of them; because God, of his sovereign grace and goodwill, determined on it; grace set wisdom at work to find out a proper way and method of making men just with God, which could never have been found out by men or angels; and having found a way to impute their sins, not to themselves but to Christ, and to impute his righteousness to them; he was *gracious, and said, Deliver them from going*

down to the pit (Job 33:24). Grace put him on calling Christ to be their surety, to bring in an everlasting righteousness for them; and it was grace in Christ to accept the call, and say, *Lo, I come to do thy will! (Ps. 40:7, 8)* one part of which was, to work out a righteousness for his people; and it was grace in God to send his Son to obey, suffer, and die for them, in their nature, that the righteousness of the law might be fulfilled in them; and it was grace in him to accept of that righteousness as if done by them, and to impute it to them freely without works, and to give them faith to lay hold upon it for themselves; and it appears the more to be an act of grace, in that they are *ungodly* whom God justifies, sinners, even some, the chief of sinners (*Rom. 4:5; 1 Cor. 6:11*).

An act of justice

2. It is an act of justice, as well as of grace: God is righteous in all his ways and works, and so in this; the law being perfectly fulfilled by Christ, the surety, both with respect to precept and penalty; justice is fully satisfied, and so God is *just, and the justifier of him that believeth in Jesus* (*Rom. 3:26*).

Universal to all the elect

3. It is universal, as to persons, sins, and punishment: as to persons, all the seed of Israel are justified; that is, all the elect of God and seed of Christ; as there was an *all* on whom judgment came to condemnation, through the offence of the first Adam, even all his natural posterity; so there is an *all* on whom the free gift by the righteousness of Christ comes, to the justification of life; even all the children of God, and offspring

of Christ, the second Adam, whose righteousness is *unto all*, and *upon all* them that believe (*Isa. 45:25; Rom. 5:18; 3:22*). And with respect to sins, they that are justified, are justified from all sins whatever; Christ has redeemed his people from all their iniquities; all are forgiven for his sake; his blood cleanses from all, and his righteousness clears and acquits them of all: and as to punishment, they are entirely secure from it, even to the least degree; they are saved from wrath; they are secure from all condemnation; they are delivered from the curse of the law; nor shall they be hurt by the second death, the wages of sin; it shall not have any power at all over them: the whole righteousness of Christ is imputed to them; a whole Christ is made to them righteousness; and in such a manner, that they are made the righteousness of God in him; and they are complete in him, are perfectly comely through his comeliness put upon them, a perfection of beauty, all fair, and without spot.

Done once for all

4. It is an individual act, done at once, and admits of no degrees; the sins of God's elect were altogether and at once laid on Christ, and satisfaction for them was made by him at once; he removed the iniquity of his people in one day, and by one sacrifice put away sin for ever; all sins were pardoned at once, upon this sacrifice offered, and satisfaction made; and the righteousness of Christ was accepted of, and imputed to his people at once. The sense of justification, indeed, admits of degrees; *The righteousness of God is revealed from faith to faith (Rom. 1:17)*; from one degree of faith to another; from a lesser, and lower degree of it, to an higher; it is gradually

that faith rises to a full assurance of interest in it, so that a man knows with certainty, that he is and shall be justified; the manifestations of it are various and different, at different times; but the act itself, as in God, is always the same, perfect and complete. Indeed, there are fresh declarations and repetitions of it, the sentence of it was first conceived in the divine mind from all eternity; it was virtually pronounced on the elect in Christ, their representative, at his resurrection from the dead; and it is afresh pronounced in the conscience of a believer, by the Spirit, and he bearing testimony to it; and it will be again notified at the general judgment, before angels and men; but justification, as an act of God, is but one, and done at once, and admits of no degrees; and is not carried on in a gradual, progressive way, as sanctification is.

The weakest and strongest believers all alike justified

5. It is equal to all, or all are alike justified, that are justified; the price of redemption, on which justification proceeds, is the same, the precious blood of Christ; even as the ransom price, and atonement money paid for the children of Israel, was the same, an half shekel for the rich and for the poor: and it is the same righteousness of Christ that is imputed to one as to another; it is a garment down to the feet, and covers the whole mystical body, the lowest and meanest members of it, as well as the more principal; it is unto all, and upon all them that believe; there is no difference, they have all the same righteousness, and the same precious faith, though not to the same degree, yet the weakest believer is as much justified, as the strongest believer; and so the greatest, as well as the smallest sinner,

though one may be justified from more sins than another, having committed more: yet one is not more justified than the other; though one man may have more faith, and more sanctifying grace than another, yet no man has more righteousness, or a more justifying righteousness than another.

Irreversible and unalterable

6. It is irreversible, and an unalterable act; it is according to the immutable purpose and grace of God, which can never be frustrated; it is part of that grace given, and one of those spiritual blessings wherewith the elect were blessed in Christ before the world began; it is one of those things which God does, and are for ever. Neither the righteousness by which they are justified, nor the faith by which they receive the justifying righteousness from the Lord, ever fail. The righteousness is an everlasting righteousness; and faith fails not; Christ is the author and finisher of it. Though a righteous man falls, he never falls from his righteousness: a man that is only seemingly and outwardly righteous, may turn away from his own righteousness, and go into a course of sin, and die; but one that is truly righteous, through the righteousness of Christ, can never turn and fall from that, nor shall ever enter into condemnation; but shall be eternally saved and glorified.

Though justified in God's sight, indwelling sin remains

7. Though by the act of justification, persons are freed from sin, and from obligation to punishment for it, sin is not thereby taken out of them. They are, indeed, so freed from it, that God sees no iniquity in them, to condemn them for it; he sees all the

sins of his people in the article of providence, and chastises for them; but in the article of justification he sees none in them; they are acquitted, discharged, and justified from all; yet sin dwells in them, as it did in the apostle Paul, who, undoubtedly, was a justified person; yea, *There is not a just man upon earth*; one that is truly righteous, in an evangelic sense, *that doeth good and sinneth not (Eccl. 7:20)*.

Justification animates believers to good works

8. Through justification by the righteousness of Christ, neither the law is made void and of none effect, nor is the performance of good works discouraged. The Law is not made void; *Do we make void the law through faith?* that is, through the doctrine of justification by faith in the righteousness of Christ; *God forbid! yea, we establish the law (Rom. 3:31)*; by presenting to it a righteousness every way commensurate to its demands, by which it is magnified and made honourable: nor does this doctrine discourage duty, but animates to it; and is to be constantly preached for this end, *That they which have believed in God, might be careful to maintain good works (Titus 3:7, 8)*.

Index to Scripture references